BUSINESS BY
THE BIBLE

Sonya L. Thompson

Oil & The Glory Publishing - Business By The Bible

By: Sonya L. Thompson

Printed in the United States of America
Printing All rights reserved

Second Edition

ISBN: 13: 978-1461187981

ISBN-10: 1461187982

Table of Contents

DEDICATION

To my wonderful husband Chris and son Aaron, both of whom are my driving force and inspiration. I love you both for always supporting me!

To my mom, I love you and thank you for believing in me and telling me "I can" no matter what my dream has been.

To my late grandmother Cora Neal. How she has impacted my life for Christ! She taught me how to just believe God. She always encouraged me to be the best. Somehow I know the Lord has shown her the results of the fruit of her labor. I love and miss her dearly.

To my Heavenly Father who entrusted me with this assignment, I am humbled and honored. May your voice be heard throughout the nations. May the anointing of your Spirit rise up from these pages to empower, prosper and encourage those whom you have called into the marketplace.

~ *Avoid Enticement* ~

My son, if sinful men entice you, do not give in to them. (Proverbs 1:10 NIV)

Entrepreneurship is a divine calling, a ministry, and an assignment of great responsibility. Having run a personal business for over eleven years, I am very familiar with the enticements we face as entrepreneurs. Therefore, it's very important to operate with the highest degree of integrity and to be a good steward over what the Lord has entrusted you with. As a Christian entrepreneur, your level of integrity directly reflects your Heavenly Father at all times - especially when you are dealing with the non-Christian community. For this reason you must always be on guard.

> Entrepreneurship is a divine calling, a ministry, and an assignment of great responsibility.

The word entice means to deceive, persuade or allure away from. There are those who will show up with the very intent and purpose of alluring or pulling you away from the path of integrity.

I have been in the vending industry for over eleven years, and at one point early on in my career in my career, a nationally known company called me and asked me to encourage a customer to order one hundred small candy machines in the Orlando, FL area. I stood to make several thousand dollars, except for the fact that I knew if the customer purchased those machines, she would not be able to get them out in the Orlando, FL market because of what we call market saturation- too many machines in the area. I shared this with the company, but they did not care and wanted me to talk the customer into purchasing the machines. If I helped them to secure the order they promised to send my telemarketing company a lot of business.

I agreed to speak to the customer, but once I spoke with her, I advised her not to purchase one hundred machines but a smaller quantity. It turns out this lady was a pastor's wife and the pastor wanted to start a small vending business to supplement his family's income! I am so thankful that the Lord sent them to me. Needless-to-say, because I told her the truth, I did not get any more business from that company. They found themselves out of business within a year because they did not operate with integrity.

Be ready to pass the test *when* the enemy comes to entice you to take advantage of others for your financial gain! Entrepreneurship does not come without some difficult and it will seem tougher when an enticement is involved. The word says enticements will come, so **do not give in to them.**

<u>Personal Assessment</u>

Is there anyone in my business circle who's trying to get me to compromise my integrity?

Am I misleading customers in an effort to enhance my financial position?

<u>Prayer</u>

Lord Jesus, if I have given in to the enticement of sinful men or misrepresented you in any way in the marketplace, I ask you to forgive me in your name. Surround me with those who have your heart and mind. Help me to operate with integrity and honesty as I represent your kingdom in this earth.

<u>Declaration of the day</u>

I declare I am submitted to Christ Jesus and I will not allow myself to be deceived, persuaded or allured by sinful men. As I submit to God, and resist the devil he must flee from me. I determine to bring glory to my Heavenly Father in the market place today.

Sonya L. Thompson

~ *My Notes* ~

_____

_____

_____

_____

_____

_____

_____

_____

_____

_____

_____

_____

_____

_____

_____

_____

_____

~ A Recipe for Success ~

My son, if you accept my words and store up my commands within you, turning your ear to wisdom and applying your heart to understanding — indeed, if you call out for insight and cry aloud for understanding, and if you look for it as for silver and search for it as for hidden treasure, then you will understand the fear of the LORD and find the knowledge of God. For the LORD gives wisdom; from his mouth come knowledge and understanding. (Proverbs 2:1-6 NIV)

Our society is inundated with information, most of it right at our fingertips. In addition, there are many well educated, knowledgeable and learned people in our society. Sometimes too much worldly information can be detrimental to our faith. But, even with all of the so called wisdom and information we have access to and possess, it pales in comparison to the wisdom found in the Word of God!

> **The Word of God must be your final authority!**

As long as I can remember there's always been a lot of talk about the poor condition of the economy, taxes, high gas prices, and the faltering stock market. Most of the news we hear is bad news and generally promotes a spirit of fear. If we are not careful we will find ourselves accepting the words of men over the Word of God. Jesus warns us in **Luke 8:18** to be careful how we hear. The ear is one of the gates which leads directly to the heart. Therefore, it's important to watch what and how you hear.

In Proverbs 2, Solomon gives us a recipe for success. He admonishes us to:

1. Accept the words of God and store up His commands.

The Word of God must be your final authority!

2. Turn your ear to wisdom and apply your heart to understanding

Listen to what the Holy Spirit has to say with the intention of doing it.

3. Call out for insight and cry aloud for understanding.

When you need help cry out to the Father and He will answer you.

4. Look for wisdom because it is a hidden treasure.

Do not quit, cave in or give up. He will speak to you through His word or through someone. He WILL answer you!

This is a recipe for success for every entrepreneur! The only way to obtain Godly wisdom is to store up the Word of God in your heart on a daily basis. By the way, *Godly* wisdom is far more valuable than money. If you get *Godly* wisdom you will get the money. If you get *Godly* wisdom, you will get the contract you are after. If you get *Godly* wisdom and learn how to apply it, you will build your business beyond your wildest dreams! Solomon had an opportunity to have anything he wanted and he chose wisdom. As a result, he was the wealthiest man in the world because Godly wisdom is the recipe for success!

Personal Assessment

Who has my ear first?

Is my ear attentive to the Word of God or am I looking for wisdom in other places before consulting

Prayer

Lord Jesus I turn my ear to your wisdom. I listen and cry out for it. Give me a wise and discerning heart that I may take dominion in the marketplace for your Kingdom.

Declaration of the day

I declare I have committed the Word of God to my heart. I set my ear to hear knowledge and understanding from the Holy Spirit today. I operate in and receive the wisdom of God to aid me in every situation.

~ *My Notes* ~

~ Honor the Lord With Your Increase~

Honor the Lord with your capital and sufficiency [from righteous labors] and with the firstfruits of all your income; So shall your storage places be filled with plenty, and your vats shall be overflowing with new wine. (Proverbs 3:9-10 AMP)

When I was a child, I noticed business people would take the first dollar they earned, put it in a frame and hang it up on the wall. I used to think that was so cool, but as I grew older, I found out this was done as a way for them to memorialize their first dollar made. This looks nice, but as Christians we are not instructed to hang up the first dollar as a memorial, but we are called to **"honor"** the Lord with the firstfruits of *ALL* of our income! This means the **"first portion"** of all of our income belongs to Him.

> Furthermore, an entrepreneur who knows how to honor the Father with their firstfruits is an EVEN more valuable asset to the kingdom of God.

The tithe and the firstfruits are two distinct acts of giving. For some reason this is a subject of great controversy in the body of Christ. I had always been taught that the firstruits offering was the same as the tithe, but this is not the case. You will find it mentioned separately and distinctly in several Scriptures. You can study this on your own by looking at: **Genesis 4:3-5; Deuteronomy 14:22-23; Nehemiah 10:38-39.** These are just a few references so take time to locate other scriptures on this subject, even in the New Testament. I assure you there is a difference.

Inherent in the calling of an entrepreneur is the assignment to gather wealth to advance the kingdom of God and fund the end time harvest. Unfortunately many successful entrepreneurs get caught up in owning things and forget the purpose of their wealth flow. Of course God wants us to live a quality life, but this can't be our first point of focus. An entrepreneur who understands the purpose of their money becomes a very valuable vessel in the hands of our God. Furthermore, an entrepreneur who knows how to honor the Father with their firstfruits is an EVEN more valuable asset to the kingdom of God.

In every stream of income or increase you receive, there is a *firstfruits offering* that must be given to honor the Lord. This will require allowing the Holy Spirit to help you identify the **first** in all of the income you receive. This offering reminds us that God is our divine source of everything and it sets the stage to bless everything else that follows.

My very first year in business I made over $100,000. I was a tither, but I knew nothing at that time about firstfruits and as a result I did not hang on to much of what I earned. I simply could not understand it. I have found out some of the laws we don't know still hurt us! A short time later I learned about and gained revelation concerning the firstfruits offering. I began to honor the Lord and the Father began to fill my storage places (bank accounts, and investments). So, my statement is not based on study alone but application with the results to follow. I encourage you to put this principle to work in your life. As you honor the Lord with your increase, He will honor you openly. Honor always gets the blessing!

Personal Assessment

*Am I honoring the Lord with the firstfruits
of all my income?*

*As the Lord increases me, am I making my finances
available for the Kingdom?*

Prayer

*Lord Jesus, give me revelation concerning the first fruit
offering. As you teach me through your Spirit, I will
honor you with the firstfruits of all my income from my
righteous labors and place your Kingdom first at all times.*

Declaration of the day

*I declare as I honor the Lord with my firstfruits offering,
my business, bank accounts, and investments are filled
with plenty and the blessing of the Lord rests on my
household. I declare I receive new ideas, insights and
concepts flowing into my life today.*

Sonya L. Thompson

~ *My Notes* ~

_____

_____

_____

_____

_____

_____

_____

_____

_____

_____

_____

_____

_____

_____

_____

_____

_____

_____

~ Watch Your Flow ~

Keep thy heart with all diligence; for out of it are the issues of life. (Proverbs 4:23 KJV)

As I read this Scripture I get a visual of our inner life literally being a river that flows out to the external. It appears the place of this flow is the heart. The heart referred to here is: your mind, will, knowledge, thinking, emotions and passions. So we can see why we are admonished to keep or guard our heart with all diligence because out of it flows the issues of life. In other words, what goes into the heart will direct the flow of your life.

> A guard prevents intruders from entering in and prevents those that are captive from escaping.

A guard prevents intruders from entering in and prevents those that are captive from escaping. The Holy Spirit will do His job to warn us when we permit unhealthy things to enter or exit our heart, but in the end it must be our decision to guard it. We have to make an intentional effort to hide the Word of God in our heart and prevent anything contrary to His Word from entering in. This is the reason why you must guard your eyes, ears and mouth because these gateways lead directly to the main gate of the heart. These gateways will ultimately affect your presence or persistence in the marketplace and your quality of life! If you want your life to flow according to God's desire and plan, then His Word and the things of God must become your priority.

I have made it a practice for years to have a CD from one of my favorite teachers on finances or business playing everywhere I go. I even sleep with an IPod and have those lessons going into my heart throughout the night. I would encourage you to do the same if you really want to have a lifestyle that depicts success and prosperity. Equipping yourself with the Word of God will prepare you for the negative distractions the enemy will send your way. When you watch your flow by planting the Word of God in your heart, you will do just what Jesus did when Satan came to tempt Him. You will do what Jesus did when people come to you with a negative report about the economy. You will do what Jesus did when you have any thought of failure. You, like Jesus will say, **"It is written!"**

Your responsibility in watching your flow, is to cast down every imagination and high thing that exalts itself against the knowledge of God. If you look at your heart like a bank account you will be careful about what enters into it. Remember whatever you deposit in it will be your only resource for withdrawal. When you sow the Word, you have an abundant supply to withdraw from. If you deposit negatives, they deplete your balance and subtract from your quality of life. This will render you ineffective in the marketplace. So, watch your flow.

Personal Assessment

What kind of reports have I allowed to enter my ears, eyes, and come from my mouth lately?

How much time do I spend reading or listening to CDs and lessons on finances and business?

Prayer

Lord Jesus, help me to be more aware I of what I permit to enter my heart. As you do so, I will watch what comes out of my mouth and what goes into my ears and eyes from this day forward.

Declaration of the day

I declare I guard my heart with all diligence. Only good things will enter my eyes and ears and proceed from my mouth. As a result, my heart flows forth with abundance, success and prosperity for the kingdom of God.

Sonya L. Thompson

~ *My Notes* ~

_____

_____

_____

_____

_____

_____

_____

_____

_____

_____

_____

_____

_____

_____

_____

_____

_____

_____

~ Be Teachable ~

I would not obey my teachers or listen to my instructors. I have come to the brink of utter ruin in the midst of the whole assembly. (Proverbs 5:13-14 NIV)

A person who puts themselves in a position to learn or expand is what we would term teachable. I am sure you have heard the saying, no man is an island. This is even more so in the market-place. If you intend to reach a prominent position in your industry, you have to allow others to teach you. Being teachable involves far more than receiving advice, but it also involves correction and instruction. This is a big problem in our society; nobody really wants to be corrected. Almost nobody wants to be taught. Many people like to teach but very few like to be taught! We have a society of know-it-alls, therefore many live very unsuccessful lives.

> The more successful you become, the more you should realize the need to be taught.

As you become more experienced in business, and reach a greater degree of success, there is a risk of thinking you are the expert who is beyond instruction. Have you ever talked to someone and they act like they already know everything you are saying, but their lifestyle does not back up the knowledge they claim to have? This is a danger zone! In my book, there is nothing worse than a person who thinks they know everything! We should NEVER stop learning. The more successful you become, the more you should realize the need to be taught.

I was a salesperson for a major home improvement company in NJ for several years. My supervisor was called the "Million Dollar" man. I still hear his words today; "Just be teachable and do exactly what I do and you will succeed". As a result of heeding his advice, I was the top salesperson in the office for many years. But, as I continued on in life, I forgot this tidbit of wisdom and thought I had all of the answers. I am not proud to say, I suffered just about every financial dilemma you can name because I did not heed advice - from the Word of God or my instructors.

When we do not listen to our teachers, we will come to the brink of ruin. Remember this, your Heavenly Father called you to be an entrepreneur because He wants you to succeed! How do you avoid failure and utter ruin? Very simple, you must remain teachable. First, allow the Holy Spirit to minister to you through the Word of God and also be willing to seek out and accept godly counsel and correction as the Father sends people to your aid. A piece of wisdom - *Instruction comes in the strangest packages so don't judge a book by its cover. Be ready to receive from whomever the Father sends to you.*

Personal Assessment

Am I teachable (be honest with yourself)?

Who is in my circle of influence that can provide me with instruction? Am I willing to receive their counsel and correction?

Prayer

Lord Jesus, I yield myself to your Holy Spirit and ask you to lead me to the way of profit and teach me in the way I should go. I accept instruction from your Word and those you position in my life to bring me godly counsel.

Declaration of the day

I declare I am teachable. As a result my steps are ordered by the Lord. I declare the Father is surrounding me with godly counsel and I willingly submit and listen to my instructors.

~ *My Notes* ~

Procrastination
~The Master Trap~

A little sleep, a little slumber, a little folding of the hands to rest— and poverty will come on you like a bandit and scarcity like an armed man (Proverbs 6:10-11 NIV).

The most subtle bandit of success and the down-fall of many entrepreneurs is the spirit of procrastination. The one who procrastinates always looks towards tomorrow and tomorrow never comes. It's the master thief of dreams, and riches. It's a blindfold that covers the eyes and blots out the vision of the future. Countless millions have been siphoned from the pockets of non-productive and immobile entrepreneurs who have fallen into its trap.

> The one who procrastinates always looks towards tomorrow and tomorrow never comes.

You might be sitting on an invention, a book, idea, business or a course and not even realize you have been given the seed to the very future you have been praying for! How many times have you said, God gave me this business idea and never moved on it? How many **God** ideas have you had and watched someone else accomplish them? You have been waiting for all the stars to line up so to speak, before you can venture out. That day will never come! Furthermore, there will never be enough time to get started. You have to make the time even if it means putting in extended hours to make it happen! If this is true of you, I hope you realize you are a victim of procrastination.

Even if you presently run a business, I want to advise you not to put off expansion. Technology is constantly changing so continue to push forward to be relevant in your industry. This was the downfall of IBM, they could not conceive the idea that the small personal computer could ever replace their large mainframe computers. Where are they now? They slept, they folded their hands and poverty and scarcity showed up to do its job. This is why the lifespan of small businesses is very short, we do not move with and adapt to the changes in the industry. Change is inevitable.

Protect the business the Father has given you. You have been graced with the task of bringing wealth into the kingdom so make it a habit to seek Him for fresh, new ideas for your business. Take time to seek wisdom on how to create a market niche for yourself. When the Lord tells you what to do don't talk about it or sit on it, move on it! As you keep this in mind, you will avoid the master trap of procrastination!

Personal Assessment

*What projects have I been putting off? How can I better
use my time to accomplish my goals?*

*What is keeping me from moving forward
in my business?*

Prayer

*Lord Jesus, forgive me if I have not acted on the ideas and
insight you have given me. From this day forward I will be
faithful with the ideas you entrust me with, in your name.*

Declaration of the day

*I declare I am empowered to accomplish the goals I have
set today. I will not be stopped. I will not be denied and I
will not be hindered. Everything I set my hands to today
will prosper and profit the kingdom.*

~ *My Notes* ~

_____

_____

_____

_____

_____

_____

_____

_____

_____

_____

_____

_____

_____

_____

_____

_____

_____

_____

_____

_____

_____

~ Stay Focused ~

My son, keep my words and store up my commands within you. Keep my commands and you will live; guard my teachings as the apple of your eye. Bind them on your fingers; write them on the tablet of your heart. (Proverbs 7:1-3 NIV)

These verses depict a man or a woman whose entire life is consumed by and focused on the Word of God. When I first started my business, my hours were extremely long. There was so much fine tuning I had to do. I had to learn how to manage my employees and how to input payroll effectively. I had to put systems in place then tweak them until the business flowed effortlessly. Face it, you will also have to put a lot of time into building and fine tuning your business. As a result, you must be on guard to prevent from neglecting the true source of your success -- the Word of God.

> You must be on guard to prevent from neglecting the true source of your success -- the Word of God.

When something is stored up, it's set aside for future use and can be withdrawn at any time. If nothing has been stored up, there is obviously nothing to withdraw from! So, creating a storehouse of the Word is essential to your success. This is done by setting time aside every single day to gain instruction form the Holy Spirit and by meditating on the Word of God. When the Word becomes special to you, when it is regarded as something more precious than gold, you will do whatever is necessary to guard your time spent meditating on it. As you begin to study and stay focused on His Word, you will find that you are living and manifesting the Word.

We are encouraged to bind the Word of God on our fingers, meaning that the work of your hands should be governed by the Word of God. Your work in the marketplace should exemplify the Word that has been stored up in your heart. Both saved and unsaved people should notice that your work ethic is different. The way that you conduct your business should grab the attention of those you serve in the marketplace.

In verse three you are encouraged to write the Word on the tablet of your heart. This means the Word literally becomes etched upon your heart. This happens as a result of meditating upon and speaking the word.

As you apply these keys, you will have a life that is focused on the Word of God!

Personal Assessment

Is the Word of God precious to me?

How much time do I spend meditating on the word and am I applying it to my life?

Lord Jesus, as I meditate upon your Word today may it be written upon the tablet of my heart, in your name.

Declaration of the day

I declare I am governed by the Word of God. I keep my mind on the Word of God today and carry out the commands of the Father in my daily activities. I yield my mind, my fingers and my heart to the Lord so He may be glorified in the marketplace.

~ *My Notes* ~

~ Obtain Riches, Honor, Wealth, Prosperity And Favor ~

With me are riches and honor, enduring wealth and prosperity. For those who find me find life and receive favor from the LORD. (Proverbs 8:18 & 35 NIV)

This entire chapter echoes wisdom's call. It's a call which never ceases. Wisdom is likened to a woman who cries out and awaits patiently for those who will respond to her voice. When I was young my mom would come out on the porch and cry out for us because we were a distance from the house. My brother and

> Wisdom is crying out for you every single day but you must recognize and respond to her voice when she calls

I would hear her voice and we would make our way home because we knew something special was waiting for us - a delicious home cooked meal or something not so nice if we took our time.

In like manner, wisdom is crying out for you every single day but you must recognize and respond to her voice when she calls Many entrepreneurs who attain wealth and prosperity in the marketplace find it is short-lived because wisdom does not continue to accompany them. The wisdom of the Word of God puts you in position to gain riches, honor, and the *enduring wealth and prosperity* that so many entrepreneurs desire. Wisdom brings with it not a living, but a life – this is the **God kind of life**. This is life to the full. This is a life that will go far beyond anything you've ever imagined! It is the life the Father has designed for you, while giving you the opportunity to use your/His resources to touch the lives of others.

Take note that wisdom is also accompanied by the force of favor. That word favor means: satisfaction, pleasure, enjoyment, and delight. These are the things the Father has in store for you as you run after and respond to the wisdom in His Word. This is the only way to truly obtain riches, honor, wealth, prosperity and favor in the marketplace! This is the only way you put yourself in a position to hear wisdom's call? Have an ear for the voice and Word of God, and for the godly influences He positions in your life.

When you respond to wisdom you should expect that she will have riches, honor, enduring wealth and prosperity waiting for you upon your return.

Personal Assessment

Am I spending enough time in the presence of the Holy Spirit to obtain His wisdom?

Are riches, wealth, honor, prosperity and favor evident in my life?

Prayer

Lord Jesus, I thank you for wisdom's call. I set my ear to hear your voice and will carry out your instruction in the marketplace. Your wisdom brings with it wealth, riches, honor, prosperity and favor -- I receive these from you today.

Declaration of the day

I declare my ear is open to wisdom's call. As I respond to the voice of wisdom, I receive riches, honor, wealth, prosperity and favor from the Lord from this day forward.

~ *My Notes* ~

~ Don't Waste Your Words ~

Whoever corrects a mocker invites insults; whoever rebukes the wicked incurs abuse. Do not rebuke mockers or they will hate you; rebuke the wise and they will love you. Instruct the wise and they will be wiser still; teach the righteous and they will add to their learning. (Proverbs 9:7-9 NIV)

When someone needs help or comes to me for instruction regarding their business or how to start up a business, I expect them to receive and act upon it. When you offer people business advice take careful note of those who put legs to the expertise and advice you have given them. In other words look for people who can take the instruction you have given and put it to work. These are the kind of individuals you want to pour your years of experience, wisdom and knowledge into. Just a note, at all costs avoid those who constantly ask for advice but

> **Time is one of the most precious commodities you possess.**

oppose the instruction you give - especially when you have proven your-self in that area!

Time is one of the most precious commodities you possess. That's why the Word tells us to redeem it. It's something that can never be replaced and it represents money; therefore you must guard it with all diligence. As you begin to show signs of success, you will find many people will seek you out for advice. But, you have to find a system to weed out the tire kickers.

How do you keep from wasting your words? Remember, those who love wisdom can receive instruction. Those who cannot receive it, who give you opposition when you deliver it, or who do not carry out that instruction are not the kind of people you want to invest your words or time in. When you teach the righteous they add to their learning. Look for those you can mentor who would like to add to their learning. You recognize these people by the simple fact that when they come to you for advice you will eventually see the fruit of your labor. Don't try to correct or pursue those who have come to you for advice and still have not acted upon it. It is the job of the mentee to seek out the mentor. Remember, don't waste your words and you will not waste your time.

Personal Assessment

Are my words and time being invested in the right individuals?

Who has come to me for business advice? Have they carried out that instruction?

Prayer

Lord Jesus, I thank you for those that you have placed in my life to pour instruction into. Give me a wise and discerning heart today so my words and my time will be productive for myself, others, and for your kingdom.

Declaration of the day

I declare I will not waste my words today. I will give my attention, time and words to those who are eager to receive them and put those words to work. I will pour into those the Father sends me and the fruit of my labor will be evident.

~ *My Notes* ~

~ No More Toiling! ~

The blessing of the LORD, it maketh rich, and he addeth no sorrow with it. (Proverbs 10:22 KJV)

If you knew there was a way to eliminate the toil from your work efforts would you take it? Well, I have good news for you! Your Heavenly Father has made it possible for you to experience the blessing - goodness, welfare, favor and prosperity without a lifestyle characterized by toiling. As we examine this Scripture we see an added benefit of the blessing without the element of sorrow. Before we can get excited about this, it is worth a second look. At first glance, we when look at the word sorrow we might immediately think the blessing comes without trouble or sadness, but the Hebrew definition of sorrow means **"no toiling."**

> **Toiling is the result of the curse.**

Toiling entered the scene in the book of Genesis when Adam and Eve sinned. As a result, God said Adam would eat by the sweat of his brow; that represents toiling. Therefore, toiling is the result of the curse. It means to struggle; it is exhausting labor; it makes gains by great difficulty. My friend you are no longer under the curse because of the shed blood of Jesus Christ!

Let me bring some balance here. Please understand I'm not saying that you don't need to work, but there is a difference between working and toiling. Your work is your assignment on this earth. It is what God has called you to do, so it should be a pleasure and should produce a fruitful lifestyle for you. In this case you are called to be an entrepreneur. It's something you should take great delight in and always see yourself doing. When you are working under the blessing of the Lord He will make you rich. He will cause you to prosper and get ahead without great difficulty, exhaustion or struggle.

People who toil hate their job or business and do it mainly for the money. Because of the blessing, you have an advantage over anyone in the marketplace who does not have this knowledge. You are the type of person who will attract opportunities and success even though there are others who might be more qualified. You will also seem to be able to handle and accomplish more without the extensive time others would have to put in.

It's the blessing, it is the benediction, words spoken over you by the Father when you came into the kingdom that will propel you towards success. He spoke words of wellness, happiness, prosperity and favor over you. You have to grasp the simple reality of work without toil because that's the way He always wanted it to be. We have been taught for so long that we must sacrifice everything in life to be successful. This is not so when you have revelation of the blessing. God has spoken success over you! The only thing you need to do to ensure your success is to stay connected with Him and receive instruction each day. As a result, there's no more toiling!

Personal Assessment

Am I trying to reach business success on my own?

Do I feel like I'm spinning my wheels and nothing is happening?

Prayer

Lord Jesus, I thank you for the blessing that makes me rich and adds no sorrow with it. I thank you Father that I no longer need to toil because I am free from the curse. You have spoken words of wellness, happiness, prosperity and favor over me and they have caused me to excel in the marketplace. I receive the blessing as a finished work for my success.

Declaration of the day

I declare the blessing of the Lord makes me rich. I receive wellness, happiness, prosperity and favor in my life. I decree and declare that I excel in the marketplace today.

~ *My Notes* ~

~ Generosity - The Pathway To Financial Prosperity ~

A generous man will prosper; he who refreshes others will himself be refreshed. (Proverbs 11:25 NIV)

Sometimes I wonder if generosity a thing of the past. In our society , we are very good at focusing on what we need and what our family needs but somehow we have forgotten about being generous to others. I grew up in a financially challenged household. A portion of our lives was spent on welfare therefore my thoughts were always focused on having the money to do what I wanted to do in life, so I could enjoy a better existence than what we were living. I saw entrepreneurship as a means to have my dreams come true. I wanted the house, the car and the nice clothes, but nowhere in my dream did I make room to be generous to others.

> **God desires for His children to have wealth to be liberal or free with it to bless others.**

I always knew I wanted to become an entrepreneur not just because of our financial situation, I just knew that was what I was called to be. After becoming a Christian, I understood that God desires for His children to have wealth to be liberal or free with it to bless others. Even if you are not extremely wealthy God expects you to be a blessing to others.

Trying to hold on tightly to what one has results when we do not recognize generosity as the pathway to financial prosperity. Many equate giving with losing but on the contrary, giving is not losing, it really is gain! A person who is generous is liberal in their giving or sharing -- they are unselfish. A generous man will flourish, prosper and be successful because he has considered the needs of others. According to Scripture, whatever you sow you will reap. I know this to be one hundred percent true; Because I am always eager to bless others and purposely look for opportunities to be a lender for the kingdom of God, I have the favor of God on my life and I am always refreshed financially.

If you look through the Bible you will see that your Heavenly Father is a giver. He set the stage and led by example when He gave you His one and only Son, Jesus Christ. This is an eternal example of generosity. Likewise, your giving has eternal value and will never leave your life because your Heavenly Father will never forget your acts of generosity. At some stage of the game your seed will circle back to you, bringing abundance and prosperity.

You have a great financial responsibility as an entrepreneur. The Father trusts and expects you to stretch the wealth He gives you beyond your household. His desire is for you to reach out and touch the lives of other people. In doing so you will unleash the force of generosity – the pathway to financial prosperity.

Personal Assessment

*How would God rate my generosity on
a scale of one to ten?*

Am I liberal to my local church?

Prayer

*Lord Jesus, I understand that I am blessed to be a blessing
until all ends of the earth are blessed.
Direct me today in my giving. Thank you for an
opportunity to display your goodness, kindness
and liberality to others.*

Declaration of the day

*I declare I am generous and I look for those the Father
wants me to bless today. The wealth He has given
me is available to others. As I allow Him to
direct my giving*

~ *My Notes* ~

~ It's OK To Be A Nobody ~

Better to be a nobody and yet have a servant than pretend to be somebody and have no food. (Proverbs 12:9)

There's something inherent in the hearts of men where we continually seek the approval of others. I have seen resumes where a minimal position has been glamorized to resemble the position of a CEO with just a few words. Many are defined by their houses, cars, clothes, and occupations. Pretending is a form of deception. For example, when I was growing up we could ride by the projects and see a few Mercedes-Benz cars parked outside which were owned by people we knew. The funny thing is that those same people did not have food and had difficulty keeping the lights turned on. They looked good until you followed them home and found out they were merely pretenders. Let me tell you this, it's okay to be a nobody in the eyes of men, rather than pretend to be someone,

> When you try to arrive before your time you will find yourself ensnared in a trap by the look of success rather than a lifestyle that is truly successful.

who dresses like, drives like, or lives like a somebody. I have heard this manner of living described by Dr. Leroy Thompson as trying to be big when little has got you.

When you try to arrive before your time you will find yourself ensnared in a trap by the look of success rather than a lifestyle that is truly successful. Pretenders usually find themselves overwhelmed in debt trying to keep up with the false image they've created.

When your Father created you, you were already somebody; So much so that He made you in His own image and likeness! The key to truly being somebody is to know your worth in and to Him. Your worth finds its originating point in Him. Your identity is in Christ alone. Because you are made like him, you are ALREADY somebody. It seems like we spend our entire life trying to prove we are successful to people who really could care less. It's not necessary because He has already proven your success and value in Christ Jesus! With this knowledge in mind, you no longer need to look to material things to validate your self-worth. Now, when the house, car, and fine clothes come along, you can enjoy them without stepping into pride. Things have us when we use them as a means of defining who we are.

If you hang out with God long enough everyone will know that you are somebody. In the meantime it's ok to be a nobody in the eyes of men.

Personal Assessment

How do I present myself to others?

Am I trying to live a lifestyle that I have not attained yet?

Prayer

Lord Jesus thank you for creating me in your likeness and image. I am somebody. My worth is not defined by the things that I have but by whose I am.

Declaration of the day

I declare I am fearfully and wonderfully made. I walk in and have been made in the image and likeness of my Heavenly Father. I am somebody because I know whose I am and acknowledge that my identity is in Christ alone.

~ *My Notes* ~

~ Watch Your Mouth ~

A man shall eat good by the fruit of his mouth: but the soul of the transgressors shall eat violence. (Proverbs: 13:2)

Physical work is not the only principle which brings success. There are a lot of folks working day and night and are still dissatisified with their life. There's this other little member that can make or break your business success and it's called the tongue. Somehow we have forgotten about the tongue. James chapter three goes into great detail about this powerful yet overlooked member of the body. Unless it is set in order with the Word of God it's fruit will destroy your future.

> There's this other little member that can make or break your business success and it's called the tongue.

What good is all of that hard work if your words do not agree with the outcome you desire? What will it profit you if you take all of your time preparing for a successful future and speak words that contradict the future you are trying to create? When we speak negative while we are working towards a goal, it's equivalent to building a house then turning around and tearing it back down. I am certain this is not the outcome you desire; but so many entreprenuers are using their tongue to sabotage their business. The ability to keep my tongue in order is why I have stayed in business for over eleven years, even through a recession, while others in my industry are long gone.

Here's a profound nugget of truth: Fruit and vegetables come from seed. I don't expect to harvest cabbage if I have not sown cabbage seed. Likewise, your words have the same power as a natural seed. You can't expect to reap from a Word seed you have not sown! A man shall eat good by the fruit of his mouth. The fruit is identified when we see the seed, not the finished product. This is why we can go to the store and by cabbage seed, and see the finished product of cabbage, even though we are just looking at the seed.

Your fruit is not determined when it shows up in the natural, it's identified when the seed of your mouth is released! You will eat good by the fruit of YOUR mouth. So, why do people say things they don't want but expect good things to show up? This is contrary to the universal law of sowing and reaping. It can't be done in the natural and certainly can't be done in the spiritual realm.

Proverbs 18:22 says **death and life are in the power of the tongue and those who love it will eat its fruit.**

There is power in your mouth so don't say things you don't want to come to pass. If you begin to agree with a negative report concerning your business or your finances, you will eat the fruit of your words. Your success in the marketplace is in your mouth! Your real work starts in your mouth! Difficult moments and hard decisions will have to be made. You might feel like you are on the edge on many occasions, but you must speak life to your business and it will flourish. You will come out on top if you watch your mouth.

Personal Assessment

What kind of words am I sowing for my future?

Am I in agreement with negative reports concerning my business or my industry?

Prayer

Lord Jesus, thank you for the creative power that is in my mouth. I will speak life and not death to my business and personal life. The words of my mouth and the meditations of my heart will be pleasing and acceptable to you today.

Declaration of the day

I declare I have been given dominion over my tongue. I speak words of life to my business and I will enjoy the fruit of it. I call customers and contracts from the North, South, East, and West. I command them to come to me now. I declare I am walking in abundance and overflow in the marketplace.

~ *My Notes* ~

~ Stay On Track ~

There is a way that seems right to a man, but in the end it leads to death. (Proverbs: 14:12 NIV)

So many decisions need to be made as an entrepreneur and everyone has advice to offer you. I have found that most of the people who want to give business advice have no traces of success in any area of their life nor do they have a successful business! On the other end of the spectrum, many tout themselves as experts in the field of business and entrepreneurship, but the pathways to success seem to vary a great deal. So who do you follow? How do you know if the decision you are making is the right one? How can you stay on track? It's crucial to be in the know of where to get sure direction.

> **Most of the people who want to give business advice have no traces of success in any area of their life nor do they have a successful business!**

Have you ever looked over a deal or investment and it was picture perfect? You know, it looks like a duck, walks like a duck, quacks like a duck but turns out to be a chicken! What you need to figure out is how to avoid a way that **seems** right but leads to destruction. You need to uncover/discover a way to stay on track, since just following in the footsteps of others or looking over a picture perfect contract is obviously not the only thing to do. Their way may not be your way. Their path may not be the path God has for you. There is only one way to ensure success every single time -- ask the Holy Spirit to guide you in your decision making.

I have been down the path that leads to destruction. There have been some contracts that I didn't turn down even when I felt that the Holy Spirit did not want me to take them. You would have thought I learned my lesson the first time! Because I couldn't get my mind off of the money to be made, those jobs ended up being a nightmare! In the end I had heartache, trouble, and a whole lot of stress that could have been avoided! You don't have to go down a path that seems right, but you can make sure you are heading in the right direction by obeying the leading of the Holy Spirit. He speaks as a still voice in your Spirit and He speaks to you through His Word. Neither of which should be ignored. God ALWAYS speaks in direct relation to His Word.

The questions to ask yourself today are: Am I on track? Am I true to the calling the Father has given me in the marketplace? Am I traveling in the direction that seems right to or am I allowing the Holy Spirit to direct my activity in the marketplace? Who is shaping the path I am traveling on each day?

I remind you of the words penned by King Solomon, "There is a way that seems right to man, but in the end it leads to death." I encourage you to stay on track today and walk in the way and on the path the Father has designed just for you. He is the best teacher and guide.

Personal Assessment

Am I on the path of success my Father has designed for me?

Have I potentially set myself in harm's way by engaging in a business deal that I should not be involved in?

Prayer

Father, thank you for making my path crystal clear today. I set my eyes on you and ask you to lead me by your Holy Spirit as I conduct business for you in the marketplace.

Declaration of the day

I declare my steps are ordered by the Lord. I choose the path of righteousness and avoid people and business dealings in which the Holy Spirit advises me as potential pitfalls to my success. I declare my path is made straight and my way is clear.

Sonya L. Thompson

~ *My Notes* ~

~ Be Failure Proof ~

Plans fail for lack of counsel, but with many advisers they succeed. (Proverbs 15:22 NIV)

Whenever I embark on a new business idea, I make it a habit to run it by several people; my husband, my spiritual dad and another good friend of mine. The reason I do this is because I have experienced so many disappointments and failures in life by ignoring the words of wisdom found in **Proverbs 15:22**. The Amplified Bible says, **"Where there is no counsel purposes are frustrated."** This literally means that your plans will shatter, or crack through. This is what causes the frustration. Now, when I have heard from God about a business idea I will not let anyone talk me out of it, but I use them as a sounding board to see how I can implement the idea and meet the needs of the people. God speaks through other people; no matter how good

> God speaks through other people; no matter how good you think your idea is, advisers are necessary for your success!

you think your idea is, advisers are necessary for your success!

The business idea that God has given you still requires you to consult advisers who will help you hone in on the vision. Now I understand that we have the Holy Spirit who does give us wisdom and guidance, but God also wants us to seek godly counsel. Godly counsel is not just people who say they are Christians. They are Christians who are aware of and who apply the Word of God in their lives. They have proven results. That my friend is what we term as godly counsel. Your advisers help you to bring the pieces of the pie together. They will point out things you did not think of or they can give you critical information and guidance you would never have discovered on your own.

Just a word of warning regarding the advisers you choose: do not share your plan or dream with negative people or yes men. You need people in your life who will be brutally honest - not critical, not jealous - but honest. And don't share your vision with people who will try and put out the fire of your dream. I once had someone very close to me tell me that my business would not succeed because a lot of people in the industry were going out of business in my particular industry. He proceeded to tell me how his friend had started the same business and went out of business in a few years. That meant absolutely nothing to me! God was the one who told me to start the business and He was the one who would ensure I stayed in business as long as I followed His instruction. Here I am hundreds of thousands of dollars later and I am still here!

Your plans will fail if you decline counsel, but you can be failure-proof when you consult many advisers. Your plans can and will succeed as you apply this wisdom to your life. You will be a powerhouse in the marketplace.

Personal Assessment

*Have I experienced success with the goals and
plans I have established?*

Do I have godly advisers to look over my plans?

Prayer

*Lord Jesus, thank you for the plans you have to prosper
me and give me an expected end. I thank you for the
godly advisers you have called by my side to aid, advise
and to counsel me in the marketplace.*

Declaration of the day

*I declare I am failure-proof because I present my plans
to godly counsel. As a result, I receive the wisdom and
direction needed to make every endeavor successful and
accomplish my God designed purpose in the marketplace.*

Sonya L. Thompson

~ *My Notes* ~

~ Just Roll It Off On God ~

Commit thy works unto the LORD, and thy thoughts shall be established. (Proverbs 16:3 KJV)

This is somewhat of a continuation of key number fifteen. Now, you've got your plan together, spoke to your advisers - everyone is in agreement and whala! You are ready to roll, right? Wrong! Too many times God gives us an idea and we begin to run after it, but we leave Him behind. This will not work! He is your partner in the marketplace.

> **Too many times God gives us an idea and we begin to run after it, but we leave Him behind.**

We are advised to commit our work to the Lord. The word commit means to roll off onto, or to trust with. We are committing to the Lord our transactions, our labor and our actions in the marketplace. Notice Solomon says when we commit our works to the Lord we roll off our labor and plans on Him, then our thoughts shall be established. This means the godly counsel you received can now be used to design your future. It also means you will be able to move on a course that is fixed, settled and prearranged. You will be able to move in a single-minded manner with the plans the Lord has given you. This is similar to someone weaving a pattern in the natural or preparing a blueprint. They do this so that they can have a guideline to follow and build upon. Being in the marketplace is no different.

When I started my business the first thing I needed was a name. I committed this to the Lord and within a day or so the Holy Spirit gave me the name for my business as I awakened from a nap. I took that name and mixed in with some other business names and spoke to some of my advisers about it. In every single case they picked the name the Holy Spirit had given me. This was my confirmation.

Always take the plan back to God, even after you speak with your advisers. The Holy Spirit who is the teacher of profit will show you the things your advisers have not seen and ensure your plans are established. When God says go for it you can't lose!

Also, I would highly advise writing down the time and date the Lord speaks to you about the plans you are proceeding with so you will not get discouraged when it looks like things are not going right. Just roll it off on God and your thoughts, will be established.

Personal Assessment

Have I entrusted God with my labor and my plans?

Are my plans established and firm in the marketplace?

Prayer

Father, I commit my labor and transactions to you today. I trust you with everything that concerns the business you have allowed me to be a steward over. I thank you for establishing my plans and thoughts today as I look to you.

Declaration of the day

I declare my purposes and plans, my labor and efforts are committed and entrusted to the Lord. The godly counsel and wisdom I have received is now woven together to produce a plan that is firm and secure.

~ *My Notes* ~

~ No Cosigning Allowed! ~

A man void of good sense gives a pledge and becomes security for another in the presence of his neighbor. (*Proverbs 17:18 AMP*)

Why in the world would I add this little nugget of truth in a book on business principles? It's here because you will be a success and soon enough you will encounter a friend or family member who is looking for a cosigner. It's possible they have no credit, poor credit or not enough credit. In **Proverbs 22:7**, the Bible says the borrower is a servant to the lender. Simply put, there is a switch of position in a lending transaction. The person who was

> The person who was your friend or your family member has now turned into your servant.

your friend or your family member has now turned into your servant. This makes for a lot of trouble for both parties!

A man lacks good financial sense when he makes a legal pledge to pay back something for another person! You have absolutely no control over the actions of others. People mean well and will promise you they will pay back the debt but in most cases you will get burned. If that person does not pay back the debt you are assuming their responsibility. If it turns your friend or family member does not pay the debt and you can't pay it, your credit score will take a hit. Furthermore, if you need to take a loan for anything, cosigning also reduces the amount that you can personally borrow. What I want you to see is your generosity can result in a damaged relationship or financial mishap if the loan is not repaid. It's better for you to give it to the person than to cause them to be your servant by making a loan to them.

Have you already cosigned for someone? Don't beat yourself up. Pray for the person so they will be able to pay their obligation. Have you already had your credit ruined because you cosigned for someone? Let this be a learning tool for you. It's over now so repent and ask the Lord to help you pay off the obligation and establish a good name with your creditors.

God does not want you to operate without good financial judgment. He's advising you through His servant not to become security for the debt of another person. Might I add, not even for your children! There is no cosigning allowed.

Personal Assessment

Have I cosigned for someone? Now that I have looked into the word concerning this, do I realize this is poor judgment?

Have I been left with a debt that I cosigned for and am I paying it off?

Prayer

Father, I thank you for this sound wisdom regarding cosigning for another man's debt. I will heed your advice and will not be pressured into being security of another man's obligations.

Declaration of the day

I declare I operate with good financial sense. I will not damage my relationships by turning my friends or family members into my servants I will not strike pledge or secure the debt of another.

~ *My Notes* ~

~ Humility, The Way To Honor ~

Before a downfall the heart is haughty, but humility comes before honor. (Proverbs 18:12)

Have you ever heard the saying He has a big head? It's really not the head that's big, but the heart that's puffed up and full of pride. Haughtiness or pride begins in the heart/mind. It is a cancerous condition of the heart and the forerunner of failure. It is the same condition that lodged itself in the heart of Lucifer - the former worship leader of Heaven. Pride was found in him and he lost his place of prominence with God.

> Haughtiness or pride begins in the heart/mind. It is a cancerous condition of the heart and the forerunner of failure.

As you reach a level of proven success in business, prepare to guard your heart against pride because with success comes the praise and adoration of men. There's nothing wrong with people commending you for your work or abilities, but there is something wrong when you internalize it to a point where it takes root in you. Almost instantly you may think, "this will never happen to me." Be careful of such comments since the Word says the heart is deceitful among all things. We must guard our heart at all costs and be prepared to cut down a haughty spirit if it rears its ugly head.

If humility comes before honor, it's safe to say you must operate with a heart and spirit of humility if you intend to run into a position of honor. True humility can only occur when you allow yourself to be taken out of view and permit Christ to have center stage. Humility goes far beyond words, it's a spiritual position you take intentionally. With that being said, it's perfectly ok to say thank you when you are praised, without being super spiritual. Remember the gifts you have and the success you have experienced come from and are a reflection of the Father. Without Him you can do nothing.

Your heavenly Father did not send you into the marketplace to have an inflated sense of you. He sent you out to magnify Him. He sent you out to be blessed and to bless the lives of others. Everything you do should always point back to and be centered around Him. If you do this He will exalt you beyond measure in the marketplace. You will find yourself in places and before great men wondering how you got there. It is at that time you can remind yourself and teach others that humility is the way to honor.

Personal Assessment

What kind of condition is my heart in? Do I think more highly of myself than I should?

Do I attribute my success to the Father, or do I think my education, expertise and skill has brought me or will bring me to a place of honor?

Prayer

Father, I thank you that every good and perfect gift comes from you. I humble myself under your mighty hand and invite you to move me into a position of honor before men.

Declaration of the day

I declare I will not think more highly of myself than I ought to. I am able to handle the praises of men without it causing me to be puffed up in my heart. As a result, my Heavenly Father moves me to a place of honor and prominence in the marketplace.

~ *My Notes* ~

~ Zeal Alone Is Not Enough ~

It is not good to have zeal without knowledge, nor to be hasty and miss the way. (Proverbs 19:2)

A zealous person is one who is enthusiastic or passionate about a certain thing, cause, dream or vision. Knowledge is understanding gained by observation of or by experience gained by participating in something. Solomon, under the inspiration of the Holy Spirit says, zeal without knowledge will cause you to miss the way. This seems to be a reigning problem in the life of many believers, we are zealous for the things of God, but we don't take time to gain the knowledge needed to succeed.

> **A lot of passionate, enthusiastic and excited people are out of business today!**

At some point in time, every entrepreneur has gone full steam ahead on some project without the knowledge needed and ended up at a dead end. Excitement is great. Passion is to be applauded. Enthusiasm is a wonderful. But, when it comes to your business you cannot expect to succeed on these things alone. A lot of passionate, enthusiastic and excited people are out of business today! Therefore, be ready to add knowledge to your zeal.

Before I started my business I worked for a company for a little over a year and gained some very valuable experience in the vending industry. I had no idea this was the industry I was going to end up in, but God knew. He put me in that position to gain the knowledge and experience I would need to have great success in this field.

I knew a pastor who opened a restaurant, and if I heard him correctly, he never worked in one before but observed the practices, menus, waitresses and operations in some of his favorite restaurants before he opened his own. This is how he gained his knowledge which he paired with his zeal. For a while he had great success. Unfortunately, his zeal took the forefront, and his business failed after a few years. Consistency is the key my friend. Never allow your business to perate on emotion.

I firmly believe that God says what He means and means what He says. Take to heart these word: Do not be hasty in your decision-making. It's necessary for you to gain the knowledge you need first before you move ahead, and as you continue – unless you miss your way. Zeal alone is not enough.

<u>Personal Assessment</u>

*Am I merely zealous about the business decisions
I am about to make?*

*Have I gathered the knowledge I need by
observation or participation?*

<u>Prayer</u>

*Father, direct me to the knowledge needed to accomplish
my mission in the marketplace. As I pair my zeal with
knowledge I will travel on the path of success and bring
glory to your name.*

<u>Declaration of the day</u>

*I declare I gather the knowledge needed before any
decisions are made. I will not act in a hasty manner
at any time. I allow my steps to be ordered by the Holy
Spirit. Therefore, I will not miss my way, but will have
success in the marketplace.*

~ *My Notes* ~

~ Lose The Lottery Mentality ~

An inheritance gained hastily at the beginning will not be blessed at the end. (Proverbs 20:21 NKJV)

Have you ever watched those documentaries on the lives of people who have won the lottery? Over ninety-five perecent are flat broke in about a year or less! Many end up divorced and find themselves living a lifestyle far from the dream they had sketched out for themselves. Some have even ended up dead.

> **When you gain something too quickly, you are less apt to appreciate and value it.**

For example, a 55-year-old man ran a successful contracting company in West Virginia when he won a $315 million Powerball jackpot. At the time, it was the biggest amount ever won by a single ticket holder. He already had a net worth of $17 million and received a $114 million check after taxes. He gave money to Christian charities and a foundation supporting low-income families. Though he did some good with his winnings, his bad deeds far outweighed them. He was arrested twice; A woman sued him after he groped her at a dog racetrack. Thieves took $545,000 in cash from his car while he was visiting a strip club. About a year later, thieves again stole $200,000 from his car. He was sued for bouncing $1.5 million in checks while gambling. Finally, his wife divorced him!

Some people just can't handle a large sum of money at one time, this is why we must mature into our wealth. You have no clue of the amount of money that will take you over the edge. When you gain something too quickly, you are less apt to appreciate and value it. It really is possible to lose your mind if you are given too much wealth at one time without the character to back it up.

Your Father desires to pour out financial abundance in your life but He will not do it too quickly. He releases it similar to a time release capsule- giving you an adequate dosage for that time in your life. As you show yourself faithful with what He has entrusted you with, He will allow greater access in this area. He will never give you access to what you can't handle, otherwise you may find yourself overmedicated on wealth and lose your passion and your purpose for Him and your assignment in the marketplace.

Your success in the marketplace is not in going to be found in a windfall because the windfall could very well be your downfall if you are not ready for it! Lose the lottery mentality and allow the Father to release you into your wealthy place a little at a time.

Personal Assessment

Am I looking for a financial windfall or do I understand that wealth is gathered little by little?

Am I content where I am right now as I press forward and allow the Lord to prosper my soul in the area of finances as I study His Word?

Prayer

Father, thank you that I will prosper as my soul prospers. Therefore, I mediate on and study your Word to step into financial abundance.

Declaration of the day

I declare I do not expect or look to gain wealth hastily. As I mediate on the Word of God and apply His principles I increase financially and walk in the abundant favors of God.

Sonya L. Thompson

~ *My Notes* ~

~ Get Up And Work! ~

Lazy people finally die of hunger because they won't get up and go to work. (Proverbs 21:25 ~MSG)

As a child I used to think if I had my own business I would not have to work. I would imagine hundreds of people working for me and my business would pretty much run itself. You might be laughing right now because you have thought this very same thing at one time. Unfortunately, much of this ideology was based on what I saw on television. I would see these

> **Never get into a mindset where you think you're done working**

millionaires who traveled all over the world spend their days eating in the finest restaurants and their evenings lying on the beach under a moonlit sky. The funny thing was, they never ran out of money and never seemed to work! I hope you realize this scenario, for the most part, is very far from the truth. At least two thirds of the millionaire community spend 45 to 55 hours per week doing what most people are running from – **working.**

When I started my own business I hired several telemarketers and allowed them to do the majority of the phone work while I tended to the sales and customer service end of things. I found out very quickly a few of those employees did not have the same heart for my business as I did, so I had to get back into the actual work part of the business to protect what God had given me.

You have to get up early in the morning, check in on your business and determine if everything is going as scheduled. Follow up on delegated tasks to ensure they are done to the highest degree of quality. Never get into a mindset where you think you're done working. As long as you have a business there will be some form of work involved. There are a lot of business people wanting and starving because they won't put the necessary hours in. The aspect of wanting and starving goes far deeper than just the needs of life; it also reflects a desire to be successful without putting in the work and for this reason they starve and want for success.

At all costs, NEVER allow yourself to become lazy in your work ethic. Do not hand your business over to people and simply think you will check in from time to time to collect your money. No smart businessperson turns their vision and future over to another person. You've been with your business and it's your responsibility to make sure everything is operating properly. Get up and work.

Personal Assessment

Do I have a set routine each day?

Am I trusting others to run my business without my guidance and observation?

Prayer

Father, thank you for the business you have given me. I will continue to be faithful and diligent in the marketplace. Thank you for the strength to rise early each day to accomplish your will and desires.

Declaration of the day

I rise early in the morning and competently carry out and oversee the events of my business. I am diligent and energetic as I approach my tasks each today.

~ *My Notes* ~

~ Recognize The Warning Signals ~

The prudent see danger and take refuge, but the simple keep going and pay the penalty. (Proverbs 22:3 NIV)

B e careful of running after every new thing that comes along. Be guarded in believing what everyone tells you about a business deal. Be cautious when it comes to following everyone who looks like they are successful. In the end those who run after every whim, will experience some kind of disadvantage, loss or suffering.

> Your success in the marketplace and your ability to glorify the Father will only be possible if you are able to recognize the warning signals.

A critical attribute which should be pursued by every entrepreneur is mentioned here- prudence. Prudence is a term we have heard used so many times, but what does it really mean to be prudent? A prudent person is skilled in good judgment, cautious of danger or risk and wise in handling practical matters.

As you operate in the marketplace endeavor to look at an opportunity from every side of the equation - not just from the side of profit. This is how you keep balance in your life and in your business and avoid the penalty spoken of. He says to take refuge or hide from danger when it is revealed to you. Do not keep going simply because on paper the deal looks sweet or because you see financial success in the person's life who is presenting it to you. It might not be for you! I think I've mentioned it before, just because it looks like a duck, walks like a duck and quacks like a duck, does not make it a duck!

Years ago I ran after an opportunity and I have to tell you, I was ruined financially. Now, I will say the person who I was dealing with falsified paperwork so my decision was affected by it. But I still should have known better! The Lord was warning me but I would not ignore the financial gain and the results were devastating. It was the most difficult time in my life.

I am convinced that wisdom and sound judgment - the character traits of being prudent can only come through the guidance of the Holy Spirit. Since my last financial disaster, I can't tell you the number of situations I have been saved from because the Holy Spirit uncovered the dangers that were ahead.

Your success in the marketplace and your ability to glorify the Father will only be possible if you are able to recognize the warning signals. This involves the ability to see danger in the natural as it is revealed to you by the

Holy Spirit and your willingness to take refuge. Miss it and you will pay the penalty.

Personal Assessment

Have I been warned by the Holy Spirit of possible pitfalls that lie ahead with any business alliance or deal I am considering or involved in?

Prayer

Father, I permit the Holy Spirit to take control of my presence in the marketplace today. I ask you to open my spiritual eyes so I can walk in prudence and avoid any pitfalls that lie ahead.

Declaration of the day

I declare I am prudent. I see and avoid dangerous alliances, contracts or relationships which the Holy Spirit reveals to me. I have a wise and discerning heart and avoid the penalties of the simple.

~ *My Notes* ~

~ Don't Be Left Empty Handed ~

Don't for a minute envy careless rebels; soak yourself in the Fear-of-God—That's where your future lies. Then you won't be left with an armload of nothing. (Proverbs 23:17-18 MSG)

From the outside It looks like the sinners or careless rebels seem to prosper and have no worries. Even our children are now looking at those who live a godless life and are wondering how these people can live the way they do and still prosper. I will let you in on a secret, In **Psalm 73:17**, David said this: **he had envied the wicked until he went into the sanctuary and he saw their end.**

> We must literally saturate ourselves with His Word in order to avoid this kind of behavior.

Jesus said, **"What does it profit a man to gain the whole world and in the end lose his soul?" Mark 8:36.**

A friend of mine who is a real estate agent worked for a broker who uses deceitful practices to sell property and to obtain listings. They strong-arm their way into deals, pushing out the smaller person. A person like this is what scripture calls a careless rebel. In the end they will be weighed in the balance and found wanting. Solomon tells us to soak ourselves in the fear of the Lord as a remedy against this type of poisonous lifestyle. One aspect of the of the fear of the Lord is to hate evil. We must literally saturate ourselves with His Word in order to avoid this kind of behavior.

You may observe people who are not serving the Lord and it looks like they're prospering, but don't compare yourself to these careless rebels. Don't worry about what they drive, what kind of house they live in or the kind of clothes they wear. If they continue on their course, in the end they will be left with an armload of nothing. They will be left empty-handed in this life and in eternity. This the determined destiny of everyone without the Lord Jesus Christ.

As much as the Father wants you to be successful in the marketplace because it brings Him glory, your future doesn't lie in that. Your future lies in keeping your eyes on Him, not on men, and accomplishing the mission He has given you. What matters more than anything is your relationship with Him. He will see to it that you have a nice home, car and so forth; but unlike your rebellious counterparts you won't be left empty-handed

Personal Assessment

Do I envy the success of the wicked?

Have I "soaked" myself in the fear of the Lord?

Prayer

Father, thank you that my lot in life is secure. Everything you have for me will be released as I soak myself in the fear of the Lord and keep my focus on you. In the end I will have a fulfilled and meaningful life.

Declaration of the day

I do not compare my successes or lack of to the godless nor will I permit envy to find a place in my heart. As I soak myself in the fear of the Lord my way is made prosperous.

~ *My Notes* ~

~ What Are You Made Of? ~

If you fall to pieces in a crisis, there wasn't much to you in the first place. (Proverbs 24:10 MSG)

TAG Heuer had a campaign some years ago entitled: **"What are you made of."** This campaign featured many celebrities. In the commercials these celebrities offered insight into their successes and values. Now, if you know anything at all about advertising you understand that the purpose was to make a connection between the celebrity, the TAG watch and YOU! It really was about translating to your subconscious mind that the watch "made you," and further would make you like them. The goal was to have you identify the celebrity and the watch as a symbol of success and believe that the TAG watch made you somebody just like Tiger Woods or Maria Sharapova.

> It's very easy to look solid and stable when everything around you appears to be going well, but what happens when you come into a moment or season of crisis?

I'll ask you this question: When you encounter trials and

difficulties in your business, "What are you made of?" I hope you realize your worth is not in the things that are external but in the One who is internal. So I ask you again, "What are you made of?"

Many Christians found out when our economy collapsed, they were not rooted and grounded in the Word of God. Fear and doubt set in their hearts because they lost their jobs or saw a decline in their businesses. As a result, many were left financially devastated. It's very easy to look solid and stable when everything around you appears to be going well, but what happens when you come into a moment or season of crisis? It is what's on the inside that's going to keep you on solid ground.

If you can only prosper when everything is going well, you have to ask yourself "What am I made of?" Do you know how to work the Word of God to create an intentional prosperous outcome? Jesus said the man who hears the Word and does it is a person who builds their house on the rock and when the winds and the waves come he will not be moved!

What you are made of, not the kind of watch you wear, will determine your success in the marketplace. The Word of God, if acted upon in faith, will cause you to prosper at any time! Then, when, not if a crisis arises, you will not fall to pieces but you'll be able to show the world what you are made of.

Personal Assessment

Do I know who I am in Christ Jesus?

Do I see myself as My Father sees me?

Prayer

Heavenly Father, thank you for creating me in your image and likeness. As I uncover my identity in you, I am able to stand in times of crisis.

Declaration of the day

I declare my worth has been established by my Heavenly Father because He has made me in His image and likeness. I am able to stand in the midst of adversity because His Spirit lives in me and I know who I am in Him.

~ *My Notes* ~

~ Put Your Confidence In The Competent ~

Confidence in an unfaithful man in time of trouble is like a broken tooth or a foot out of joint. (Proverbs 25:19 AMP)

Have you ever broken a tooth before or had a joint out of place? I have and what a painful experience that was. Solomon says if we put our confidence in an unfaithful man, a person who is disloyal or untrustworthy during times of trouble, it'll be just as painful as having a broken tooth or a joint out of place!

> **Because many people are looking for a paycheck, it's going to be difficult to put the right people in place to support your vision.**

Have you ever noticed that the busiest person in the office always seems to attract the most work? It's because the business owner or manager has confidence in the competence of that person, based on their past performance. They know the job will get done.

It's important for you to have people working for you whom you can have confidence. If the ones you employ don't fit the bill. I would highly suggest you replace them. You can't expect to have success in the marketplace if you surround yourself with people who lack quality of character.

Of all the people I have employed, one lady who stood out from the crowd was a lady by the name of Wilma. She had great respect for me and was able to connect with the mission I wanted to accomplish in my industry. If I gave her an assignment I never had to worry if it would be completed in a timely manner or with excellence. When she passed away it was devastating to me, not only because she had become a close friend, but I knew she was a diamond in the rough and would be nearly impossible to replace.

Because many people are looking for a paycheck, it's going to be difficult to put the right people in place to support your vision. Your goal should be to surround yourself with people who will make you and your Heavenly Father look good in the marketplace. Never hire people just to fill a position! The first thing you should always do is ask the Holy Spirit if this is a person to add to your staff. While you await your answer check out their background and find out how they served their previous employer. If you can't have confidence in their competence, do not hire them.

Those who are unfaithful will turn out to be as painful as a broken tooth or a foot out of joint in your time of trouble. Put your confidence in the competent.

Personal Assessment

Do I have employees or volunteers around me who I am confident in?

Am I willing to make the changes needed as the Holy Spirit directs me?

Prayer

Heavenly Father, I put my trust in you alone. I lean not to my own understanding but acknowledge you before I hire any employee or staff member. I rely and depend on your guidance through the Holy Spirit.

Declaration of the day

I declare the Spirit of the Lord leads me in every decision today. I will not depend merely on their qualifications, but will allow Him to give me the discernment needed to add to my staff.

~ *My Notes* ~

~ Get Past The Obstacles ~

The slothful man saith, There is a lion in the way; a lion is in the streets. (Proverbs 26:13 KJV)

Slothfulness or laziness is a cousin to procrastination because it is the putting off or postponement of a journey or mission until... A person who is slothful has a tendency to avoid situations which require them to go beyond the norm to get the job done. If it is easy they'll go after it, but if it looks like it's going to take some extra effort he or she will begin to make all kinds of excuses as to why they can't accomplish their dreams or goals.

> I believe your answer to overcome any obstacle you are facing or will face has already been learned.

On another note, what amazes me, is how the emergence of social media has become an obstacle which is robbing people of their future. Some spend hours on Facebook, Twitter, Instagram and so forth. At some point other platforms will emerge and demand even more of their time and attention. They literally spend hours per day reading about everyone else's life and posting pictures of themselves instead of perfecting and running after their own future! If you ask them why they haven't accomplished their goals they'll tell you they don't have the time! These platform are making for a slothful culture of individuals.

The fact that you are reading this book tells me you are not slothful but are a person who desires to learn and apply the wisdom found in the Word of God.

I have spoken with entrepreneurs over the course of the years and in conversation they'll offer a reason why they never pursued the God given vision placed in them. What they concentrate on is all of the reasons why they can't succeed. They are immobilized by the fear of failure; like those who watched Goliath as he taunted the Israelite army day after day, and all they could see was the nine foot obstacle in their way!

Desire to be like David and learn how to formulate a strategy to maneuver your way past it. Do not focus on the obstacle; yes you know it's there, but your focus should be on getting past it. Somewhere in your life's journey you have learned many life lessons. I believe your answer to overcome any obstacle you are facing or will face has already been learned. David pulled from his memory and experience when he fought the lion and the bear. In his mind that was enough to get past Goliath, and gain the financial reward that was associated with defeating him!

Regardless of the obstacle you face, your Heavenly Father has already equipped you to overcome it. Allow the Holy Spirit to show you how to draw from your prior experiences and give you the wisdom needed to get past it today.

"For the diligent a week has seven days; for the slothful a week has seven tomorrows"

- German Proverb -

Personal Assessment

What obstacles am I facing or believe I will face as I establish my business in the marketplace?

Prayer

Heavenly Father, I thank you in advance for the courage to overcome every obstacle I may face. I thank you for wisdom and a sound mind and the experience I have already had that will lead me into victory.

Declaration of the day

I declare I have been equipped by my Father to overcome every obstacle. I will not be hindered or distracted by the what I am experiencing or what lies ahead. I will not quit but will be victorious.

Sonya L. Thompson

~ *My Notes* ~

~ Know Your Financial Condition ~

Be sure you know the condition of your flocks, give careful attention to your herds. (Proverbs 27:23)

I wish someone would've told me about this Proverb ten years ago! At first glance one only thinks of flocks such as goats and cows and so forth. But we have to be skilled enough to take the Word of God and make it relevant to our lives today. You probably don't have flocks (well maybe you do). But you have a business, and money and investments. In this text lies a principle of assessing or knowing your financial condition at all times to keep you prepared for the future.

> Assessing or knowing your financial condition at all times will keep you prepared for the future.

The very first year I emerged into the marketplace, I made over $100,000. Yes, I made it and I spent it! Now

I'm not saying I did anything bad with the money. I tithed and was very generous to various ministries, but I did not take time to evaluate my financial condition. I had so much money coming in each week, I found myself neglecting to balance my checkbook some weeks, until I ended up spending payroll money and having far less in my account than I thought! At the end of that first year, when I went to my accountant and had my taxes prepared I came to the conclusion I did not know the condition of my flocks. This was my wake-up call! From that point to this day, I make sure my checkbook is balanced on a daily basis. At all times I know what my assets are and where they are located. I am aware of what is to be used for investing, advertising, debt repayment, tax purposes and for living. I never base tomorrow's expenditures on today's success because business sales fluctuate. We can't speculate on our success but must take time to plan and prepare for the future. Be very careful in taking care of your flocks and paying attention to your herds.

You will have ups and downs in the marketplace and unforeseen expenditures which will arise. Can I offer you some sound advice? Know how much money you are bringing in and how much is going out. You should have some type of financial plan written up that covers everything from investments, taxes, inventory, savings, expenses and so forth. Find yourself a good accountant who is abreast of the latest tax laws. Make it your business to balance your checkbook at least three times per week. This is the most valuable advice I can give you. If you do these things you will find yourself rising to another level financially as you manage the state of your flocks, and give attention to your herds.

Personal Assessment

Do I have a written personal plan?

Do I have a qualified accountant to help me keep my financial affairs in order?

Do I keep my checkbook balanced on a regular basis?

Prayer

Father, grant me the wisdom to manage my financial affairs. It is my desire to honor you in the marketplace as I handle wealth for your Kingdom. Aid me in finding the help I need to stay organized financially.

Declaration of the day

I declare I walk in financial wisdom and surround myself with the people and resources needed to monitor the condition of my finances. I am an active participant in my financial future.

Sonya L. Thompson

~ *My Notes* ~

_____

_____

_____

_____

_____

_____

_____

_____

_____

_____

_____

_____

_____

_____

_____

_____

_____

_____

_____

~ Faithfulness = Prosperity ~

A faithful man shall abound with blessings: but he that maketh haste to be rich shall not be innocent. (Proverbs 28:20 KJV)

It's really tough to find faithful people in today's society, especially in the marketplace. Everyone is preoccupied with running after their dream of being successful and wealthy. This verse says a *faithful* man shall abound with blessings. Anybody can be faithful for a little while but the faithfulness referred to here is a person who is steady, stable and trustworthy ALL OF THE TIME. This type of person will increase, multiply and prosper in the blessings of God.

> People who love money are hasty to become rich. It is the love of money, not money that causes so many to error in the faith.

Your Heavenly Father made a promise to those who can remain steady, trustworthy and stable; you will abound with His blessings. Continue to set priorities and stick with them. Develop a daily routine. Be faithful to your clients, faithful to your calling, steady and stable in gathering wealth for the Kingdom; then you will abound in blessings. The blessing of the Lord brings happiness, wellness, favor, and prosperity. It's available in every area of your life but faithfulness is the requirement to take part in this promise.

Now there is a flipside to this promise; the person who is hasty to be rich shall not go unpunished for their deeds. There is a penalty to pay when we attempt to become wealthy at the cost of others. A person who is hasty to be rich will do anything to get money.

Believe it or not, I once had a Christian businessman tell me he would do anything for money! Within one year this gentleman ended up hurting a lot of people, losing his insurance license and the last I heard, was facing jail time as a result of his actions!

1 Timothy 6:10
For the *love of money* is the root of all evil: which while some coveted after, they have erred from the faith, and pierced themselves through with many sorrows.

People who love money are hasty to become rich. It is the *love of money, not money* that causes so many to error in the faith. Be faithful and walk worthy of the calling the Father has given you. As a result you will abound in blessings because **faithfulness = prosperity**.

Personal Assessment

*Have I proven to be faithful with my assignment
in the marketplace?*

Am I hasty to become wealthy?

Prayer

*Heavenly Father, I desire to be faithful in the marketplace.
More than anything, help me to be committed to you
along with your purposes and
plans for my life.*

Declaration of the day

*I declare my heart is committed to the Lord. I am faithful
in all the Father has entrusted to me. I am not hasty to
become rich nor will I jeopardize others for my financial
gain. I declare my faithfulness leads me to true prosperity.*

~ *My Notes* ~

~ Take Care Of The Poor ~

The good-hearted understand what it's like to be poor; the hardhearted haven't the faintest idea. (Proverbs 29:7 MSG)

I grew up in Paterson, New Jersey in an area that became a rundown drug infested gang zone after some time. I always wondered why we were poor. As I grew older I realized we weren't really poor; in fact we had more than most people in our area, but had a poverty mindset and misused what God had given us. This is not the type of poor being referred to here. He is talking about people who are *genuinely poor,* not people who have the means to take care of themselves but use their money in a way that is not productive for their household.

> Some people have never had to do without anything in their lives and therefore they do not have a heart that is tender for those who are truly in need.

Many ministries have lent themselves to taking care of those who are truly poor. One that comes to mind very quickly is Feed the Children. I am not endorsing this charity, it's just one that comes to mind as I write this book. This is a ministry that takes care of feeding and meeting the needs of children right here in the United States. The level of poverty in the United States never ceases to amaze me, especially since this is the land of plenty. Our Father expects us to take the wealth He gives us- whatever degree that it is, and use it to take care of the poor. Some people have never had to do without anything in their lives and therefore they do not have a heart that is tender for those who are truly in need.

As you begin to increase in wealth and as you are established in the marketplace, make a decision to connect with a valid ministry that supports and takes care of the poor. That ministry may be right in your church; they may have an outreach program for the poor. If not, find a ministry which is actively meeting the needs of those who are hungry, and those who are in need of clothing, or shelter. As always you should have an ear for the Lord to help the poor you encounter on a daily basis.

In Matthew 25, Jesus said **whatever you do for the least of these, you have done for me**. Only the hardhearted resist giving to those who are truly poor.

Please be aware of those who tell you they are poor but are really people who have misappropriated what God has given them. It is not your job to take care of everyone, but it is your responsibility to be led by the Holy Spirit and use your resources to lift up the heads of those who are less fortunate. Never get to a point where you forget about what it was like before you got to where you are today. Remember, to take care of the poor.

Personal Assessment

Am I actively giving into a ministry that supports the poor?

Do I have a heart for those that are less fortunate than I am?

Prayer

Father, your Word says as I give to the poor I lend to the Lord. I will remain tender-hearted toward those who are less fortunate than I am. As I give to the least of these, I do it unto you.

Declaration of the day

I declare I am tender-hearted to those who are genuinely poor. I fulfill the Father's mandate to feed, clothe and shelter the poor. Holy Spirit, direct me to a ministry which supports your desires and purposes in this area.

Sonya L. Thompson

~ *My Notes* ~

~ Know When To Say No ~

The leech has two daughters, crying, Give, give! There are three things that are never satisfied, yes, four that do not say, It is enough. (Proverbs 30:15 AMP)

I don't know about you, but leeches are really creepy looking to me! I remember a picture of this slimy little creature sucking the blood from a person's arm or leg as it was used for medical treatment on television. The leech has two daughters: give and give. This means the beggar is never satisfied. The one with a leech-like mentality wants more and more

> The one with a leech-like mentality wants more and more without any input or accountability!

without any input or accountability! Now let's look at how you can apply this nugget of wisdom to your life.

As the Father moves you up the ladder of financial success you will find there are family members and friends who are waiting to meet you at the top with their hands stretch out. As you will see, the leech comes in many forms. It can be a brother, sister, best friend, old acquaintance or even a child. Generally this person has an entitlement mentality and expects you to give to them because you have reached financial success and are associated with them. Because you have it they feel they should have it. Certainly there's nothing wrong with giving to family members or your friends, but you have to know when to say no.

Let me give you a warning, you will not be popular when you tell them no. The most common response to your no will be "I know you can spare that one hundred dollars. You make plenty of money, what is that to you?" The leech's most valuable weapon is the spear of guilt which he aims directly at your heart. They also will pull the, If you were a Christian card, without notice! If I received one dollar every time I heard these responses, I would have been a millionaire a long time ago.

The best thing that you can do for a person is to teach them how to be successful. Teach them how the Kingdom of God works so they can apply His financial laws to their own life. If you continue to give in to the cry of the leech, it will never stop until *you* are left empty. Remember, you are not your brother's or your sister's source - God is their source. Be sensitive to the Holy Spirit because after all, the resources God has given you really don't belong to you anyway. He has entrusted you with them to advance His Kingdom and to be a blessing to those He leads you to; so know when to say no!

Personal Assessment

Have I allowed my family members or friends to
continually use me as their financial source?

Prayer

*Heavenly Father, help me to guard the wealth you have
given me and give me the insight to recognize those who
are using me for their financial gain. Forgive me if I have
allowed other to make me their source instead of you.
Show me how to help them step into the life you have for
them.*

Declaration of the day

*I declare I know when to say no. I have a wise and
discerning spirit and am able to identify those who are
draining me financially. I will permit the Holy Spirit to
direct me to give when the Father tells me to.*

Sonya L. Thompson

~ *My Notes* ~

_____

_____

_____

_____

_____

_____

_____

_____

_____

_____

_____

_____

_____

_____

_____

_____

_____

_____

~ The Virtuous Woman ~

Proverbs 31 (AMP)

I have always loved the description of the virtuous woman as recorded in Proverbs thirty-one. One thing I quickly realized after reading it was: this is who I wanted to be. From verse eleven to the end of this chapter we see a vivid picture of a woman who has it all together. Verse eleven says this virtuous woman's husband trusts in and believes in her.

> She is not caught up in the affairs of everyone else because she is too busy fulfilling her divine assignment!

Verse twelve says she comforts, encourages, and does him only good as long as there is life within her. This chapter is loaded with the attributes that every woman should strive to possess and every man should desire in his wife.

She brings in food for the family; She is a worker; She comforts and encourages; She provides for her family. She opens her mouth with wisdom and speaks with kindness. She is crafty with her hands; She is not a gossip; She is an entrepreneur! Her children respect her and speak well of her; She reverently worships and fears the Lord. Wow, what a woman! This should be the benchmark for every woman who reads this book. Men, this is the woman the Father has for you! Set the standard high, seek her out, and He will deliver. A woman like this by your side will help you reach your life goals.

Do these women exist? Yes they do and there are many in the making. These women have set their standard of achievement according to this chapter. Ladies, if we pattern our lives after this chapter, we will shine in our homes and in the marketplace and have a fulfilled life. Notice that this woman minds her own business. Yes, I had to say it! She is not caught up in the affairs of everyone else because she is too busy fulfilling her divine assignment!

Ladies I would advise you to meditate on this chapter every day and covet these attributes. In the end, you will be transformed into a thing of beauty.

Single men, keep Proverbs thirty-one before you so you will desire and recognize the wife the Father sends into your midst.

Husbands declare these attributes about your wife every day and watch how He transforms her right before your eyes!

The Bible says, beauty is fleeting, but the woman described here in Proverbs thirty-one is a rare find - a jewel.

Personal Assessment

Ladies: *How many of these attributes do I possess? What are those I am lacking and what needs to be improved upon?*

Men: *How many of these attributes does my wife possess? Which of these is she lacking? Which need to be improved upon?*

Prayer

Ladies: Father, I desire to be the virtuous woman you have described in Proverbs thirty-one. As I meditate on your Word, I thank you for transforming me into a thing of beauty in my home and in the marketplace.

Men: Father thank you for my wife. Rather than reminding her of how she does not meet the standard, I will declare the attributes of Proverbs thirty-one over her (begin to declare those areas over her life).

Declaration of the day

I declare I am/she is a virtuous woman who reverently worships and fears the Lord. I am/she is not a gossip but encourage(s) and comfort (s) those around me/her. When I/she open (s) my/her mouth wisdom and kindness are the result.

Sonya L. Thompson

~ *My Notes* ~

Do You Know Jesus as Your Lord and Savior?

The Lord Jesus Christ has an awesome plan for your life! He has already paid the price for your sins. If you will invite Him into your heart and life today, you will begin to walk in the destiny He has designed just for you.

Pray This Prayer Out Loud:

Heavenly Father, I ask you to forgive my sins. I believe Jesus is the Son of God. He died on the cross for my sins and was raised from the dead. I invite Jesus Christ into my heart and life to be my Lord and Savior today. Fill me will your Holy Spirit. Thank you Jesus for shedding your blood for me and for making me part of your family. I commit my life to you from this day forward.

Welcome to the family of God! I would love to hear from you if you made Jesus your Lord and Savior!

inof@oilandtheglory.com

ABOUT THE AUTHOR

Born in Paterson, New Jersey, Sonya L Thompson is an ordained minister. She has always had a burning desire to be a successful entrepreneur. She is involved in the vending, and financial services industries. Sonya holds a B.S. in the field of Business Administration. She has been a Christian for over 25 years and has a passion to connect people to the Living God. Her desire is to see the body of Christ become manifestors of the Kingdom of God, in order to draw the unsaved to the Father. Her calling is to **"Train, Educate and Advise through the Gospel with Simplicity and Purity."**

Made in the USA
Las Vegas, NV
17 July 2024

92462077R10095